AN EARLY LEARNER BOOK

COUNTING
1·2·3

Written by M.C. Leeka
Illustrated by Chris McDonough

Modern Publishing
A Division of Unisystems, Inc.
New York, New York 10022
Series UPC #49605

1-one   1-one

One gorilla at the zoo

1-one   1-one

One policeman dressed in blue

2-two 2-two 2-two

Two little kittens asleep
in a chair

2-two 2-two 2-two

Two young girls with curly hair

3-three 3-three

Three tall glasses filled
with milk

3-three 3-three

Three ladies' dresses made
of silk

4-four   4-four

Four rabbits hopping down
the path

4-four 4-four

Four little birds taking a bath

5-five 5-five 5-five

Five kites flying high

5-five 5-five 5-five

Five slices of cherry pie

6-six 6-six 6-six

Six piglets in a pen

6-six 6-six 6-six

Six lions in a den

7-seven 7-seven

Seven puppies being fed

7-seven 7-seven

Seven bakers baking bread

8-eight 8-eight

Eight castles made of sand

8-eight 8-eight

Eight boats approaching land

9-nine 9-nine

Nine cookies on a plate

9-nine 9-nine

Nine apples in a crate

10-ten 10-ten

Ten swans on the lake

10-ten   10-ten

Ten candles on a cake

odd odd odd

1

3

7

odd odd odd

5

9

even even even

2

4

8

even even even

6

10